प्रेम करते चलो

A Moment with Myself

A JOURNAL TO TAP INTO YOUR INNER WISDOM

Ayushi Bhawsar

INDIA · SINGAPORE · MALAYSIA

ISBN
Paperback 979-8-89724-781-3
Hardcase 979-8-89744-962-0

Contents

Note to the Reader

This journal is a bridge to reconnect with yourself. In the rush of everyday life, it's easy to lose touch with our thoughts, emotions, and inner wisdom. But today, by picking up this journal, you are creating a space to slow down and meet yourself with kindness.

This journal gently guides you on a journey of self-reflection, moments of joy and an acknowledgment of your strength. Through simple yet meaningful exercises, you'll cultivate positive emotions, set intentions for your days and embrace your authentic self without judgment.

There is no right or wrong way to go through this journal. Move at your own pace and let your thoughts flow freely. This is your space, your time, your journey.

A Few Gentle Guidelines:

Approach this journal with openness and pure intention.

Begin your sentences with "I" or "I am" to affirm your thoughts.

Write as if you are experiencing the moment now.

Let your emotions flow without judgment.

Visualize each scenario to make it personal and meaningful.

Note: Intention | Bhava:

Our intentions and attitude are powerful forces in everything we do. Our intentions define our destiny. Read, remind, and repeat your intentions every day.

You are beautiful
inside out

Welcome!
Your inner journey begins now
We'd love to hear your story in a creative way!
Tell us what brought you here!
Share something about your personality and your life philosophy
Without using your name

Faith is all we need to move forward

Your faith brought you here. Everything is possible when we believe in ourselves and the Supreme Power.

Intention of the day

I trust myself and the higher reality.

I believe I can do this.

I am ready to move forward.

I have faith in the higher reality.

I am faithful.

Reflection

Do you remember the first time you stood on your own 2 feet or rode a cycle/bike? That moment when, all of a sudden, it just clicked? What gave you the courage to find your balance?

Once again, we need to remind ourselves...

" I Can "

What is one special gift you believe God has blessed you with?

What is one unique talent you were born with?

What is one thing in your life that others often appreciate you for?

What is one thing about yourself that makes you feel proud?

Do you remember that one subject in primary school that always seemed the hardest to pass? What was it?

How did you overcome your fear of that subject to ensure you passed?

One life decision you've made purely on a leap of faith?

Morning self-care routine

Forgive yourself for 2 things that bring feelings of regret

Express gratitude for 2 things that worked in your favor yesterday

Appreciate yourself for 2 things you successfully accomplished yesterday

Think about 2 tasks that have been long pending. Let's motivate ourselves to accomplish them today.

I choose to complete_______________________________________

I am ready today to_______________________________________

Day 1

Night self-care routine

Sit comfortably on the floor with your legs crossed, keeping your eyes closed. Watch your entire day as a movie, from start to end, seeing everyone as a character, including yourself.

What are the 3 joyful highlights of your day?

What food did you eat from morning to night?

Recollect 3 emotions or moods from morning to night.

Day 1

We admire you
for prioritising yourself

Here, your journey begins! We accept you with all your qualities and flaws, with all your strengths and weaknesses. First step on the path begins with acceptance.

Intention of the day

I accept myself and my present reality.

I accept all my emotions as a part of me.

I allow myself to feel the way I feel.

I release all the blockages from my mind and body.

I am ready to release my pain.

Activity

Look around and choose any simple object, shape, or plant of your choice, and draw it on the right side of the box below.

Now, draw the same thing on the left side with your opposite hand.

Day 2

Is your left half as active as the right? or vice versa. Remember, it's still a part of you. When your right hand engages your logical mind, your left hand sparks your creative mind. Embrace and accept all of yourself!

What is the one thing this activity made you realize about yourself?

What was your favorite video game in childhood?

What was the most joyful part of that game?

One thing you would like to gift yourself from your childhood?

Let's scroll through our phone gallery and choose 3 moments where you fully accepted yourself.

Reflect deeply and make it your wallpaper today.

Day 2

A gift of forgiveness

Think of a person whom you misunderstood at some point.

Recall one memory with this person that brings a feeling of regret.

It's okay! Are you ready to mentally and emotionally say sorry to them? Just do it!

A self-realization is equal to forgiveness.

Choose one thing for which you would like to forgive yourself.
I choose to forgive myself for

Think about 2 tasks you find difficult to complete. Let's condition ourselves to accomplish them today.

I believe I can____

I know I am able to____

Day 3

As children, we all used to live in our inner wonderland, and we had our own ways of perceiving the world.

Do you remember your childhood toy? What did you name it?

What was your favorite way to spend time in your inner wonderland?

What was your hobby in childhood?

Name one person who made learning joyful for you.

Choose any 3 people you would like to thank for shaping your childhood.

Morning self-care routine

Follow your heart and choose 2 thing to pamper yourself

Express gratitude for 2 things that worked in your favor yesterday

Thank you time!
Recall 2 things for which you are truly thankful.

Think about 2 tasks you find difficult to complete. Let's condition ourselves to accomplish them today.

I believe I can____

I know I am able to____

Day 3

Night self-care routine

Sit comfortably on the floor with your legs crossed, keeping your eyes closed. Watch your entire day as a movie, from start to end, seeing everyone as a character, including yourself.

What are the 3 joyful highlights of your day?

What food did you eat from morning to night?

Recollect 3 emotions or moods from morning to night.

Day 3

Your presence is so gentle and kind!

We have achieved so much in life; now it's time to embrace and honor our accomplishments with gratitude and pride.

Recall 5 small things from yesterday that you were able to accomplish

Intention of the day

I am ready to experience warmth and gentleness.

I am ready to unlock the loving energy within myself.

I choose empathy and love for myself.

I allow my feelings to flow freely.

I allow myself to experience inner happiness today.

The feather touch is all you need!
Hold the tail of feather and feel it on your skin.

Write 3 feelings you experience.

Feather touch feel

What is the one thing you would choose to do to pamper yourself today?

What is that one food item that mentally transports you back home?

Which is that one childhood TV show that made you laugh?

Morning self-care routine

Forgive yourself for 2 things that bring feelings of regret

Express gratitude for 2 things that worked in your favor yesterday

Appreciate yourself for 2 things you successfully accomplished yesterday

Think about 2 tasks that have been long pending. Let's motivate ourselves to accomplish them today.

I choose to complete_______________________________________

I am ready today to_______________________________________

Day 4

Night self-care routine

Sit comfortably on the floor with your legs crossed, keeping your eyes closed. Watch your entire day as a movie, from start to end, seeing everyone as a character, including yourself.

What are the 3 joyful highlights of your day?

What food did you eat from morning to night?

Recollect 3 emotions or moods from morning to night.

You are glowing with confidence

Kindness is the best gift we can offer ourself today.

Intention of the day

I choose to be kind to myself.

I am ready to express my emotions to myself.

I choose kindness in difficult situations.

I forgive myself as well as others.

I can see good in everything.

Activity

We all have one person in life who stretches our boundaries or makes us angry. It's time to see them as a movie character. Recall 5 good qualities you see in them. It's time to forgive the friction and embrace their authenticity.

Day 5

Let go of your anger, irritation, and pain, and organize your thoughts.

Fill the boxes below with different patterns as you organize your thoughts in your mind.

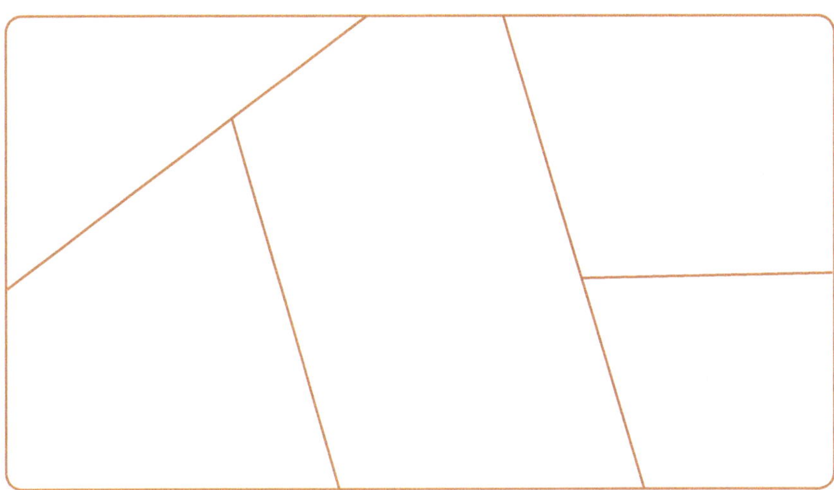

Let's welcome 3 positive feelings for today.

Morning self-care routine

Forgive yourself for 2 things that bring feelings of regret

Express gratitude for 2 things that worked in your favor yesterday

Appreciate yourself for 2 things you successfully accomplished yesterday

Think about 2 tasks that have been long pending. Let's motivate ourselves to accomplish them today.

I choose to complete_______________________________________

I am ready today to_______________________________________

Day 5

Night self-care routine

Sit comfortably on the floor with your legs crossed, keeping your eyes closed. Watch your entire day as a movie, from start to end, seeing everyone as a character, including yourself.

What are the 3 joyful highlights of your day?

What food did you eat from morning to night?

Recollect 3 emotions or moods from morning to night.

We adore your dedication toward self

It's time to revive our childhood and reconnect with our school days

Sit comfortably on the floor, gaze outside, and play a song from your childhood. Let the music fill your heart with warmth and nostalgia

> *Reflection*

What feeling does this song bring to you?

What is one thing you truly appreciate about the old times?

If there is a door that opens to your school days, Whom do you meet first?

One thing you found unique about yourself as a child?

One growth you see in yourself now?

We all had that one personalized landscape in our drawing book, a special place that felt like our own world. Let's draw it now and let the memories flood back.

Write a small message to your younger self

Morning self-care routine

Follow your heart and choose 2 thing to pamper yourself

Express gratitude for 2 things that worked in your favor yesterday

Thank you time!
Recall 2 things for which you are truly thankful.

Think about 2 tasks you find difficult to complete. Let's condition ourselves to accomplish them today.

I believe I can____

I know I am able to____

Day 6

Night self-care routine

Sit comfortably on the floor with your legs crossed, keeping your eyes closed. Watch your entire day as a movie, from start to end, seeing everyone as a character, including yourself.

What are the 3 joyful highlights of your day?

What food did you eat from morning to night?

Recollect 3 emotions or moods from morning to night.

Day 6

Your consistency toward self is courageous

It's time to free ourselves from all the baggages

Intention of the day

I free myself from all past experiences.

I free myself from all expectations.

I remove all blockages from my body and mind.

I release the baggage of heavy emotions.

I am ready to let go of pain and negative emotions.

Activity

Sit cross-legged on the floor, hold your left wrist with your right hand behind your back.
Slowly, while exhaling, bow down and breathe normally in the posture for 20 seconds. Inculcate the feeling of letting go, releasing, and relaxing.

Release all your emotions below through scribble

One of your favorite chocolates from your childhood that
no longer exists in the market.

One bad habit you have improved with dedication.

The last time you cried in silence.

One thing you choose to give away from your surroundings.

Which emotion are you ready to release today?

Day 7

Morning self-care routine

Forgive yourself for 2 things that bring feelings of regret

Express gratitude for 2 things that worked in your favor yesterday

Appreciate yourself for 2 things you successfully accomplished yesterday

Think about 2 tasks that have been long pending. Let's motivate ourselves to accomplish them today.

I choose to complete_______________________________________

I am ready today to_______________________________________

Day 7

Night self-care routine

Sit comfortably on the floor with your legs crossed, keeping your eyes closed. Watch your entire day as a movie, from start to end, seeing everyone as a character, including yourself.

What are the 3 joyful highlights of your day?

What food did you eat from morning to night?

Recollect 3 emotions or moods from morning to night.

You've successfully developed the strength to deal with challenges

It's time to unlock the treasure of potential, break the patterns of weakness, and untangle the knots of discomfort.

Intention of the day

I am strong enough to deal with challenges.

I am wise enough to solve problems.

I have the courage to face obstacles.

I am calm and stable in every situation.

Activity

Let's follow the rhythm of our heart and trace it on paper with a small challenge.

Draw something below without using your hands. Hold the pen with your mouth, let the music fill your soul, and allow your heart to guide every stroke.

What is one thing you learned from the most difficult situation?

What is your favorite board game, sport, or art form?

What does it teach you?

What is one thing you've done in life that you never imagined?

Think about one of your inner strengths that makes you stronger.

Day 8

Morning self-care routine

Follow your heart and choose 2 thing to pamper yourself

Express gratitude for 2 things that worked in your favor yesterday

Thank you time!
Recall 2 things for which you are truly thankful.

Think about 2 tasks you find difficult to complete. Let's condition ourselves to accomplish them today.

I believe I can___________________________________

I know I am able to_________________________________

Day 8

Night self-care routine

Sit comfortably on the floor with your legs crossed, keeping your eyes closed. Watch your entire day as a movie, from start to end, seeing everyone as a character, including yourself.

What are the 3 joyful highlights of your day?

What food did you eat from morning to night?

Recollect 3 emotions or moods from morning to night.

Day 8

We are amazed to see the fearless version of you

We witness you becoming stronger every day, and it's time to choose courage once again.

Intention of the day

I am ready to listen to my inner self now.

I am courageous enough to face my fear.

I am ready to accept my truth.

I free myself from all baggage and limitations.

Visualization

Imagine 2 versions of yourself behind separate windows one, the fearful version, and the other, the fearless one. Embrace them both, for they are a part of you. Both versions are worthy of love and understanding.

Write a message to both the version of you

Day 9

If God offered to grant one wish, what would you ask to be
fulfilled?

What would you choose if you could travel to your past and
fulfill one lack?

What is one skill you wish you had learned in the past to
help your personality bloom?

Do you have any phobias? What is the core fear behind that?

Are you willing to overcome it?

Day 9

Morning self-care routine

Forgive yourself for 2 things that bring feelings of regret

Express gratitude for 2 things that worked in your favor yesterday

Appreciate yourself for 2 things you successfully accomplished yesterday

Think about 2 tasks you find difficult to complete. Let's condition ourselves to accomplish them today.

I believe today I can______________________________________

I am able to_____________________________________today

Day 9

Night self-care routine

Sit comfortably on the floor with your legs crossed, keeping your eyes closed. Watch your entire day as a movie, from start to end, seeing everyone as a character, including yourself.

What are the 3 joyful highlights of your day?

What food did you eat from morning to night?

Recollect 3 emotions or moods from morning to night.

Day 9

Your inner warmth is blissful

We have all grown financially and are living in aesthetic homes, yet we still remember that one tiny, cozy home where we lived in the warmth of love, the art of adjustment, and the comfort of coziness.

Do you remember your comfort home?

Recall your time living in that home and write 5 things that made the experience so beautiful and warm.

Reflection

What is one thing you would like to carry from that home?

What is one soft skill you learned from someone while living with them?

What is one thing you cherish in your current living?

Close your eyes and see yourself in that time. What were the inner qualities that defined you during that era?

Morning self-care routine

Forgive yourself for 2 things that bring feelings of regret

Express gratitude for 2 things that worked in your favor yesterday

Appreciate yourself for 2 things you successfully accomplished yesterday

Think about 2 tasks that have been long pending. Let's motivate ourselves to accomplish them today.

I choose to complete_________________________________

I am ready today to_________________________________

Day 10

Night self-care routine

Sit comfortably on the floor with your legs crossed, keeping your eyes closed. Watch your entire day as a movie, from start to end, seeing everyone as a character, including yourself.

What are the 3 joyful highlights of your day?

What food did you eat from morning to night?

Recollect 3 emotions or moods from morning to night.

Day 10

We are happy to see the polite version of you

From today onwards,
I am ready to transform my anger into compassion.

Intention of the day

I am now harmless to myself and others.

I choose to be kind and polite in any situation.

I choose to see the positive in everything.

I am aware of my words, thoughts, and actions.

Visualization

When we are violent, we lose clarity. It's time to declutter our minds and regain that clarity.

Imagine that the shapes below are our thoughts. Gently organize them in separate compartments, bringing clarity and peace to the chaos within.

Day 11

We all have one person who brings disturbance or violence to our thoughts. It's time to reflect on a few good qualities of their personality.

Now the power is in our hands. Mention 5 things you are capable of seeing in them.

I choose to forgive myself for_______________________________

I choose to be kind on___________________________________

I choose to be non-violent on_______________________________

Today onwards, choose Non-violence (Ahimsa) as your superpower throughout the day.

Experience after the end of the day

Were you able to remind yourself to choose non-violence?

One thing you experience about yourself while practicing non-violence.

One feeling that defines your day.

One difficulty you've experienced.

One personal gain with the practice of non-violence.

Today onwards, choose Non-violence (Ahimsa) as your superpower throughout the day.

Night self-care routine

Sit comfortably on the floor with your legs crossed, keeping your eyes closed. Watch your entire day as a movie, from start to end, seeing everyone as a character, including yourself.

What are the 3 joyful highlights of your day?

What food did you eat from morning to night?

Recollect 3 emotions or moods from morning to night.

It's time for Honesty Hour!

Honesty is an investment that comes back with surprising returns. Are you ready to invest in this policy?

Intention of the day

I accept my truth.

I am ready to be truthful with myself.

I am strong enough to listen to myself.

I am wise enough to choose my words.

Honesty Test

One strength of yours that helps in survival.

One weakness of yours that pulls you down.

One deepest truth you've shared with someone.

One lie you told someone about yourself.

What comforted you to be truthful with them?

What fear or doubt made you lie?

One thing that makes you feel proud of yourself.

One thing that makes you feel guilty about yourself.

One thing you've learned about yourself just now.

One thing you've realized about yourself just now.

One blessing you would like to give yourself today.

One thing you would like to forgive yourself for today.

Draw 5 things that flash in your mind one after the other (close your eyes and see).

Today onwards, choose Truth (Satya) as your superpower throughout the day.

You surely deserve a treat for your courage and honesty.

Choose a self-care or self-grooming activity for yourself today that makes you feel warm, cozy, and confident.

I choose to pamper myself with

One dish you choose to have that mentally transports you to your comfort place.

Appreciate yourself for any 5 things.

Day 12

Write your experience below after the day ends.

What have you discovered about yourself today?

One fear that still makes you lie.

What has this practice taught you?

**Today onwards, choose Truth (Satya)
as your superpower throughout the day.**

Day 12

You have successfully unlocked the potential within you

YYou stole our hearts, and we want them back! Because we appreciate non-stealing.

Intention of the day

I am the witness of my actions.

I am always aware.

I am ready to follow non-stealing.

I am ready to bring honesty into all my actions.

I respect people's time, effort, and hard work.

Activity

Draw a mirror image of the scenery above with your less dominant hand. Be honest, and no cheating. Remember it's not about perfection it's about honesty toward self.

Day 13

How many things have you kept that belong to someone else?

Have you ever stolen other people's time through small lies? Recollect.

Have you ever taken credit for someone else's work unknowingly?

It's okay to forgive yourself and mentally apologize to all of them.

I am ready to return _________________which belongs to

_______________________________.

I apologize to ____________________for stealing

their_______________________________.

Today onwards choose Non-stealing (Asteya) as your superpower throughout the day.

Day 13

Experience

One feeling you've experienced with this practice.

One thing you've learned about yourself.

One inner gift you've received from this practice.

One blessing you like to give yourself?

To Do List

I choose to do________________________________today

I am focus to________________________________today

I believe I can________________________________today

I know I am ready to________________________today

Day 13

Night self-care routine

Sit comfortably on the floor with your legs crossed, keeping your eyes closed. Watch your entire day as a movie, from start to end, seeing everyone as a character, including yourself.

What are the 3 joyful highlights of your day?

What food did you eat from morning to night?

Recollect 3 emotions or moods from morning to night.

Day 13

Game-changing year

One thing you are truly blessed with.

One thing you are grateful for.

One thing you are joyful about.

Write below 3 keywords that define your ambition for 2025.

Bigger victory starts with a small resolution;
let's aim to celebrate a small win for the day.

I am focus today to _______________________________

I am ready today to _______________________________

I believe today i can_______________________________

I know I am ready to_______________________________

Day 14

We have achieved a lot in life; it's time to
embrace our accomplishments.

Recall 5 small things you accomplished yesterday.

Close your eyes and write the first 5 things
that flash in your mind.

Day 14

Your inner beauty is outshining

It's time to comfort ourselves in the discomfort.

One food item that is pleasurable to your taste buds.

One fragrance you are deeply indulged in.

One visually pleasing thing that has the potential to consume your time.

One cosmetic product that convinces you to spend money.

One thing you spend money on to please yourself.

You are now aware of your weakness; it's a good place to be aware.

Day 15

Are you consuming these things, or are they consuming you?

Today, let's choose to take control of our senses.

Intention of the day

I am ready to take control of my senses.

I choose to eat mindfully.

I am focused on drawing my senses inward.

I make healthy choices before consuming anything.

I am always aware.

I make healthy choices for myself.

Activity

Sit comfortably, close both ears with your fingertips, and gently close your eyes. Now, try to listen to the sounds inside your body. Focus completely for 5 minutes.

Write down one thing you choose to consume mindfully today.

Today onwards, choose to follow Self-control (Brahmacharya) as your superpower throughout the day.

Practice

One food craving you choose to resist willingly today.

One comfort you choose to avoid willingly today.

One feeling you choose to get detached from.

One willpower you are ready to experience today.

Choose any sensory organ you like to give rest today (eyes, ears, tongue).

You are learning the art of letting go

We all have a personalized treasure box of things we like to collect. Do you remember yours?

What was that one thing you enjoy collecting?

What was that one feeling you experience every time you add to your collection?

Are you willing to give away something from your collection?

What is one thing in your surroundings that occupies a lot of space (your belongings)?

Do you need them or want them?

It's time to release certain things, thoughts, and emotions.

I am ready to let go of excessive things, thoughts, and emotions.

I choose to give away whatever exceeds my needs.

I choose to free my space.

I am ready to release control.

I am ready to experience clarity.

Activity

Organize your stuff so that 50% of the space is filled with shapes and 50% remains empty.

I choose to giveaway_________________________today

I choose to let go_____________________________today

Today onwards, choose to follow Non-greed (Aparigraha) as your superpower throughout the day.

Experience

How do you feel after letting go?

One new thing you've experienced about yourself.

What do you find difficult to let go of?

Let go of one thing mentally that you feel you can't live without.

One blessing for yourself today.

Your discipline is truly inspiring

It's time to appreciate our small wins. List 5 positive changes you saw in yourself in the last 5 days.

Reflection

Mention below any 3 feelings you experienced yesterday in chronological order.

Mention below any 3 feelings you would like to experience today.

Day 17

Our brain is intelligent and creative enough to connect the dots.
Connect the dots below in a creative manner to form a design of your choice.

What is the one thing you choose to do for yourself today?

Your Aura is now cleaner and purer

A clean space reflects a clear mind,
and a clear mind creates a peaceful space.
Are you ready to experience the clarity?

Intention of the day

I am ready to clean my space, mind, and thoughts.

I choose cleanliness as my superpower today.

I am ready to experience clarity today.

I choose to remove all blocked energy and negativity.

Imagination

Observe the image below with complete concentration and tell us 5 emotions that this image evokes in you.

Kyuki Har Tasveer Kuch Kehti Hai...

One act that makes you feel energetic and active.

One person who silently motivates you to be a better version
of yourself.

One person who makes you feel accepted and heard.

One thing in your surroundings that needs cleaning.

One act of hygiene or purity you choose for yourself today.

One clarity of thought you would like to experience today.

Today onwards, choose Purity (Shaucha)
as your superpower throughout the day.

Day 17

Contentment is the key to inner happiness

When we try to do too much, we become restless. It's better to tell ourselves, 'It's okay'.

Intention of the day

I enjoy and cherish what I have.

I accept my capabilities today as they are.

I am happy and peaceful with everything I have.

I choose to feel calm and content.

Activity

Release all your emotions below with abstract scribbling art.

One food dish that brings joy to your heart.

One food dish that reminds you of your school lunchtime.

One act you choose to relax yourself today.

One heavy emotion you are ready to release today.

Tell us 3 things you have in sufficient quantity for survival.

Tell us 3 things you are highly content with.

Today onwards, choose Contentment (Santosh) as your superpower throughout the day.

Your self-control is leading to success

*Let's bow down to the teacher inside you.
Touch your forehead to the ground and thank
your own self for all the learning.*

This reminds me that we all had one favorite teacher in
our childhood with whom we loved to learn.

What is one thing you like about your favorite teacher?

What was that one quality of theirs that inspired you to
learn from them?

What is that one thing you wished you had learned in your
childhood?

Do you believe your teacher exists within you through their
teachings?

*Close your eyes and say thank you to your
teachers.*

Day 19

Draw any 3 things that you used to draw in your drawing book or the last page of your notebook.

Imagine your teacher can read this
Write a small gratitude letter to your teacher.

Your self-control is surprising

Our self-discipline makes us self-sufficient.

I am ready to choose self-discipline.

I am ready to practice self-control.

I am ready to witness my actions.

I am ready to experience my willpower.

I am faithful and strong.

There is big difference between

I can do it	I have to do it
Hope	force
Will power	Rigidity
Faith	Aggretion
Ahimsa	Himsa
Sattva	Rajas

Everything we do as Tapa should be followed
by faith and willpower.

Activity

Stand on one leg, bring your palms together before your chest,
and allow yourself to experience self-control for one minute.

Ekpadasana

One thought that shakes your balance.	One thought that keeps you steady.
One struggle you face within yourself.	One thing you've learned by yourself.

What is one thing you do willingly every day without fail.

Tell us about one habit that you improved with dedication.

One thing you do for yourself every day religiously.

We all have a tendency to fall into unhealthy habits because of our comfort zone, as they provide pleasure, right?
But have you ever experienced the victory of overcoming those habits? It's time now!

Day 20

One thing that always draws you into the trap of the comfort zone.

One thing you want to follow but are unable to apply.

What is one thing you would like to improve about yourself but find difficult to achieve?

What is one thing that gives pleasure and trouble at the same time?

Choose one thing to practice today as self-control.

Choose one thing to practice today as self-discipline.

Today let's inculcate inner strength through Mental Mauna.

Take control of your thoughts and embrace the silence within your mind. Whenever you notice the chatter in your mind, remind yourself that you are fasting today. Sssshhhhh!!!

Day 20

Night self-care routine

Sit comfortably on the floor with your legs crossed, keeping your eyes closed. Watch your entire day as a movie, from start to end, seeing everyone as a character, including yourself.

What are the 3 joyful highlights of your day?

What food did you eat from morning to night?

Recollect 3 emotions or moods from morning to night.

Outer world is the mirror of the inner world

Name a person with whom you find yourself:

Joyful

Peaceful

Energetic

Adventurous

competitive

Irritated

dishonest

Anxious

Think deeper; what similarity do you find in them and yourself? It's a good way to study ourselves.

Whom do you fear losing the most?

One emotional comfort this person provides to you.

One thing that makes you dependent on them.

Intention of the day

I choose to study myself.

I am ready to witness my actions and emotions.

I am ready to experience every cell of my body.

I am ready to listen to my body.

Activity

Do you like mountains?
Let's experience the world from a mountain's perspective.

- Sit cross-legged, firm, and steady on the ground.
- Join your palm above your head in a mountain pose.
- Stay in this posture for 2 min.
- Deeply observe each part of your body and feeling.

Describe one discomfort or feeling you've experienced just now.

*Today onwards, choose Self-study (Svadhyaya)
as your superpower throughout the day.*

Day 21

We've now reached the
path of surrender

To experience the sense of upliftment,
we must learn to bow down and surrender.

*What are the top 5 accomplishment of life that
have filled you with pride and a sense of fulfillment?*

From your birth till now. Start your sentence with 'I...'

-

-

-

-

-

Well done!!

Now recall each phase of your achievement, one
by one. Recognize the role of every individual
who played a supporting part in your story,
whether positively or negatively, as they helped
you reach your target.

Now replace 'I' with **God has chosen me to** in each
sentence.

Tell us the top 5 moments of your life that gave you a sense of failure and sadness.

From your birth till now. Start your sentence with 'I'...

•

•

•

•

•

You are brave!

Now, take a moment to reflect deeply.
How have your failures played a role in shaping your achievements?

Isn't it true that everything happens for a reason, and God is taking care of us every second?

The sense of doership and worry slow the progress of inner growth. Let's do our part and trust the Supreme Power with the results.

Ishwarapranidhana
Surrender to the will of God

Sankalpa

I am now completely faithful to God.

I am ready to surrender to the will of God.

I let go of all my worries and doubts.

I trust the plan of the Universe.

I am ready to work without expectation.

What is the one self-realization you have by the end of this journey?

We would love to hear about your experience and feedback. Please scan the QR code below and share your thoughts with us.

Continue journaling and self-talk with a positive attitude and positive intention. Intention defines our destiny.

Gratitude!

I would like to pay my deepest gratitude and love
to the pure knowledge of Yoga.

I am deeply grateful to Maharishi Patanjali for
compiling the pure knowledge of Ashtanga Yoga.

I am thankful to The Yoga Institute for preserving
the purity of yogic knowledge, where I began to
learn how to apply yoga in daily life.

I am grateful to Mrs. Saloni Suri, with whom I learned
the brain rewiring technique.

And a big thank you to my parents, my family
and Myself.